HomeBuilders *Couples Series*®

building
Teamwork
in Your Marriage

By Robert Lewis
and David Boehi

*"Unless the Lord
builds the house,
its builders
labor in vain"*
(Psalm 127:1a).

FAMILYLIFE™
Bringing Timeless Principles Home
Little Rock, Arkansas

Group
Loveland, Colorado

Group's R.E.A.L. Guarantee® to you:

This Group resource incorporates our R.E.A.L. approach to ministry—one that encourages long-term retention and life transformation. It's ministry that's:

Relational
Because learner-to-learner interaction enhances learning and builds Christian friendships.

Experiential
Because what learners experience through discussion and action sticks with them up to 9 times longer than what they simply hear or read.

Applicable
Because the aim of Christian education is to equip learners to be both hearers and doers of God's Word.

Learner-based
Because learners understand and retain more when the learning process takes into consideration how they learn best.

Building Teamwork in Your Marriage

Copyright © 2001 Robert Lewis and David Boehi

Visit our Web site: **www.grouppublishing.com**

Credits
FamilyLife
Editor: David Boehi
Assistant Editor: Julie Denker

Group Publishing, Inc.
Editor: Matt Lockhart
Creative Development Editor: Paul Woods
Chief Creative Officer: Joani Schultz
Copy Editor: Bob Kretschman
Art Directors: Jenette L. McEntire and Helen Harrison
Cover Art Director: Jeff A. Storm
Computer Graphic Artist: Stephen Beer
Cover Photographer: FPG International
Illustrator: Ken Jacobsen
Production Manager: Peggy Naylor

Unless otherwise noted, Scripture taken from the HOLY BIBLE, NEW INTERNATIONAL VERSION®. Copyright © 1973, 1978, 1984 by International Bible Society. Used by permission of Zondervan Publishing House. All rights reserved.

ISBN 0-7644-2239-1
18 17 16 15 14 13 12 11 10 9 8   10 09 08 07 06 05 04

Printed in the United States of America.

How to Let the Lord Build Your House
and not labor in vain

●

The HomeBuilders Couples Series®: A small-group Bible study dedicated to making your family all that God intended.

FamilyLife is a division of Campus Crusade for Christ International, an evangelical Christian organization founded in 1951 by Bill Bright. FamilyLife was started in 1976 to help fulfill the Great Commission by strengthening marriages and families and then equipping them to go to the world with the gospel of Jesus Christ. The FamilyLife Marriage Conference is held in most major cities throughout the United States and is one of the fastest-growing marriage conferences in America today. "FamilyLife Today," a daily radio program hosted by Dennis Rainey, is heard on hundreds of stations across the country. Information on all resources offered by FamilyLife may be obtained by contacting us at the address, telephone number, or World Wide Web site listed below.

Dennis Rainey, Executive Director
FamilyLife
P.O. Box 8220
Little Rock, AR 72221-8220
1-800-FL-TODAY
www.familylife.com

A division of Campus Crusade for Christ International
Bill Bright, Founder and President

About the Sessions

Each session in this study is composed of the following categories: Warm-Up, Blueprints, Wrap-Up, and HomeBuilders Project. A description of each of these categories follows:

Warm-Up (15 minutes)

The purpose of Warm-Up is to help people unwind from a busy day and get to know each other better. Typically the first point in Warm-Up is an exercise that is meant to be fun while introducing the topic of the session. The ability to share in fun with others is important in building relationships. Another component of Warm-Up is the Project Report (except in Session One), which is designed to provide accountability for the HomeBuilders Project that is to be completed by couples between sessions.

Blueprints (60 minutes)

This is the heart of the study. In this part of each session, people answer questions related to the topic of study and look to God's Word for understanding. Some of the questions are to be answered by couples, in subgroups, or in the group at large. There are notes in the margin or instructions within a question that designate these groupings.

Wrap-Up (15 minutes)

 This category serves to "bring home the point" and wind down a session in an appropriate fashion.

HomeBuilders Project (60 minutes)

 This project is the unique application step in a HomeBuilders study. Before leaving a meeting, couples are encouraged to "Make a Date" to do the project for the session prior to the next meeting. Most HomeBuilders Projects contain three sections: (1) As a Couple—a brief exercise designed to get the date started; (2) Individually—a section of questions for husbands and wives to answer separately; and (3) Interact as a Couple— an opportunity for couples to share their answers with each other and to make application in their lives.

In addition to the above regular features, occasional activities are labeled "For Extra Impact." These are activities that generally provide a more active or visual way to make a particular point. Be mindful that people within a group have different learning styles. While most of what is presented is verbal, a visual or active exercise now and then helps engage more of the senses and appeals to people who learn best by seeing, touching, and doing.

About the Authors

Robert Lewis is a teaching pastor and directional leader at Fellowship Bible Church in Little Rock, Arkansas. He has been featured on national radio broadcasts *FamilyLife Today* and *Focus on the Family*. Robert's study of marriage and family issues has led to several books, including *Rocking the Roles* and *Raising a Modern-Day Knight*. His "Quest for Authentic Manhood Series" is used by men's groups across the country. He and his wife, Sherard, have four children.

David Boehi is a senior editor at FamilyLife, a division of Campus Crusade for Christ. He is editor of the HomeBuilders Couples Series and has written or co-written several books, including *I Still Do: Stories of Lifelong Love and Marriage* and *Preparing for Marriage*. He and his wife, Merry, live in Little Rock, Arkansas, and have two daughters.

Contents

Introduction 8

A Word About Building Teamwork 11

Session One: The Basis of Teamwork 13

Session Two: Equal, Yet Different 25

Session Three: Following Christ's Example.....................35

Session Four: Biblical Responsibilities 45

Session Five: Biblical Responses 61

Session Six: Making Teamwork Work 73

Where Do You Go From Here? 87

Our Problems, God's Answers...91

Leader's Notes 101

Introduction

When a man and woman are married, they stand before a room of witnesses and proclaim their commitment to a lifetime of love. They recite a sacred vow "to have and to hold...from this day forward...to love, honor, and cherish...for better, for worse...for richer, for poorer...in sickness and in health...as long as we both shall live."

It's a happy day, perhaps the happiest in their lives. And yet, once the honeymoon ends, once the emotions of courtship and engagement subside, many couples realize that "falling in love" and building a good marriage are two different things. Keeping those vows is much more difficult than they thought it would be.

Otherwise intelligent people, who would not think of buying a car, investing money, or even going to the grocery store without some initial planning, enter into marriage with no plan of how to make that relationship succeed.

But God has already provided the plan, a set of blueprints for building a truly God-honoring marriage. His plan is designed to enable a man and woman to grow together in a mutually satisfying relationship and then to reach out to others with the love of Christ. Ignoring this plan leads only to isolation and separation between husband and wife. It's a pattern evident in so many homes today: Failure to follow God's blueprints results in wasted effort, bitter disappointment, and, in far too many cases, divorce.

In response to this need in marriages today, FamilyLife has developed a series of small-group studies called the HomeBuilders Couples Series.

You could complete this study alone with your spouse, but we strongly urge you to either form or join a group of couples studying this material. You will find that the questions in each session not only help you grow closer to your spouse, but they help create a special environment of warmth and fellowship as you study together how to build the type of marriage you desire. Participating in a HomeBuilders group could be one of the highlights of your married life.

The Bible: Your Blueprints for a God-Honoring Marriage

You will notice as you proceed through this study that the Bible is used frequently as the final authority on issues of life and marriage. Although written thousands of years ago, this Book still speaks clearly and powerfully about the conflicts and struggles faced by men and women. The Bible is God's Word—his blueprints for building a God-honoring home and for dealing with the practical issues of living.

We encourage you to have a Bible with you for each session. For this series we use the New International Version as our primary reference. Another excellent translation is the New American Standard Bible.

Ground Rules

Each group session is designed to be enjoyable and informative—and nonthreatening. Three simple ground rules will help ensure that everyone feels comfortable and gets the most out of the experience:

1. Don't share anything that would embarrass your spouse.

2. You may pass on any question you don't want to answer.

3. If possible, plan to complete the HomeBuilders Project as a couple between group sessions.

A Few Quick Notes About Leading a HomeBuilders Group

1. Leading a group is much easier than you may think! A group leader in a HomeBuilders session is really a "facilitator." As a facilitator, your goal is simply to guide the group through the discussion questions. You don't need to teach the material—in fact, we don't want you to! The special dynamic of a HomeBuilders group is that couples teach themselves.

2. This material is designed to be used in a home study, but it also can be adapted for use in a Sunday school environment. (See page 103 for more information about this option.)

3. We have included a section of Leader's Notes in the back of this book. Be sure to read through these notes before leading a session; they will help you prepare.

4. For more material on leading a HomeBuilders group, get a copy of the *HomeBuilders Leader Guide*, by Drew and Kit Coons. This book is an excellent resource that provides helpful guidelines on how to start a study, how to keep discussion moving, and much more.

A Word About Building Teamwork

Congratulations on your decision to make building teamwork a priority in your marriage. During this study, you will be challenged to consider how you can best function as a team in your marriage.

Building teamwork requires more than one study such as this can address. The process of building teamwork involves improving communication, resolving conflict, growing together spiritually, and more. But this course is an important step in this ongoing and rewarding pursuit.

This course will address the following teamwork issues:

- What is the foundation of teamwork?

- How can our differences be a strength?

- What role does servanthood play in marriage?

- What biblical responsibilities do husbands and wives have?

- How should we respond to one another's key responsibilities?

- How can the principles of teamwork be put into practice?

We promise some stimulating conversations, and we pray that each of you will have the ability to approach this topic with a fresh and open mind as we examine what the Bible says about teamwork in marriage.

Robert Lewis and David Boehi

The Basis of Teamwork

God's Word provides the foundation upon which
teamwork in marriage is built.

W A R M • U P   15   M I N U T E S

A Team Sport

Take turns introducing yourselves and answering one
or two of the following questions:

- What is a team, group, or organization that you
  really admire? Why?

- What is a team that you follow? Why do you support this team?

- What has been one of the best teams, clubs,
  groups, or organizations you have been a part of?
  Explain what made being a part of that team a
  good experience.

- If you were to compare marriage to a team sport,
  what sport would you choose and why?

Getting Connected

Pass your books around the room, and have each couple write their names, phone numbers, and e-mail addresses.

_____

NAME, PHONE, AND E-MAIL

_____

NAME, PHONE, AND E-MAIL

_____

NAME, PHONE, AND E-MAIL

_____

NAME, PHONE, AND E-MAIL

_____

NAME, PHONE, AND E-MAIL

_____

NAME, PHONE, AND E-MAIL

_____

NAME, PHONE, AND E-MAIL

BLUEPRINTS   **60 MINUTES**

If you have a large group, form smaller groups of about six people to answer the Blueprints questions. Unless otherwise noted, answer the questions in your subgroup. After finishing each section, take time for subgroups to share their answers with the whole group.

A Winning Team

Although a married couple does not compete for a prize against other couples, in many ways a husband and wife constitute a team that battles against forces that tear at their marriage.

1. What elements are necessary to create a

winning team in sports like baseball, basketball, soccer, or football?

2. Why do teams with outstanding players sometimes lose to teams whose individual players have lower levels of athletic skill?

3. What factors can cause a team, even a good team, to not play up to its potential? Which of these factors also affect marriage?

4. What are some typical challenges couples face in marriage that require teamwork?

The Winning Edge

To build a winning team in marriage, a husband and wife must hold fast to a few key foundational convictions. Without these biblical principles, they will not operate well as a team and will grow isolated in their relationship.

The first of these principles is a prevailing theme of the New Testament: Christ-like love. Christ demonstrated this love and calls us to it.

5. Each couple should select one of the following passages. Read the passage with your spouse, and discuss how these verses about love relate to marriage. Then read your passage to the group and relate your insights.

- Matthew 22:34-40
- John 13:34-35
- John 15:12-13
- Romans 13:8-10
- 1 Corinthians 13:1-3
- 1 John 4:10-12

6. According to the passages that were just read:

- What standard of love are we called to and by whom?

- Who are we to demonstrate this love toward? Why?

- How is this love—the love of Christ—different from the love that many marriages typically experience?

7. How do these passages challenge you in relation to the love you have for your spouse?

HomeBuilders Principle:
The first foundational element in building teamwork in marriage is loving your spouse as Christ loves you.

Foundational Goals

A successful team also must set goals—it must know what it wants to accomplish. But the team must choose these goals wisely.

8. Pretend you are the coach of a youth league soccer team. As you look at your players, you see that you have a typical assortment: A couple of players are very good athletes, a couple of others look as if they may never kick a ball straight the entire season, and the rest are average.

In separate groups of men and women, discuss the following questions.

• *Men:* What do you think would happen if the only goal you gave your team was "to have fun"? How might this goal affect your practices? your players' attitudes? your players' performance during the season?

• *Women:* What do you think would happen if the only goal you gave your team was "to win the league championship"? How might this goal affect your practices? your players' attitudes? your players' performance during the season?

After discussing these questions, share your answers with the other group. Then brainstorm together a list of some good goals for a youth league soccer team to have.

Answer questions 9 and 10 with your spouse. After answering, you may want to share an appropriate insight or discovery with the group.

9. What are some goals you have for your marriage? Try to record two or three goals. Be specific. You may also want to consider which, if any, of the soccer team goals can apply to your marriage.

10. Evaluate the goals you just wrote down. What is good or bad about each goal?

11. In the Sermon on the Mount, Jesus talks about what is important in the kingdom of God and challenges his followers to choose a path quite different from that followed by most people. Read Matthew 5:14-16 and 6:25-26, 33. What does Jesus say about the goals we should set for our lives?

12. How do you think it would affect your marriage if you both sought to fulfill these goals with your whole heart?

HomeBuilders Principle:
The second foundation of a successful team in marriage is a shared purpose for your lives—serving God.

Read Ecclesiastes 4:9-12 and discuss these questions:

- What are some ways "two are better than one"?
- What is a story from your marriage that illustrates this?

Leader: After completing the Wrap-Up activity, close this session with prayer, and encourage couples to Make a Date for this session's Home-Builders Project before they leave.

Make a Date

Make a date with your spouse to meet before the next session to complete the HomeBuilders Project. Your leader will ask at the next session for you to share one aspect of this experience.

DATE

TIME

LOCATION

As a Couple [10 minutes]

Working separately, each of you should spend three minutes trying to build a house of cards. Build the tallest structure you can. At the end of three minutes, compare structures. Then, starting from scratch, spend another three minutes trying to build the tallest card structure you can. But this time, work with your spouse to build one house. After time expires, discuss these questions:

> For this "As a Couple" activity, you will need a stack of cards, such as business cards, playing cards, or index cards.

- Which structure was taller—the house you built alone or the house you built together?

- What advantage was there in working together?

Individually [20 minutes]

1. What is one way the group session challenged you to be a better teammate to your spouse? What are you going to do about this?

---

2. In which areas of your marriage do you need teamwork? Write down one of two challenges you are facing.

3. What are some things that keep your marriage team from reaching its potential?

4. What are one or two things that typically happen in your marriage when you don't work together as a team?

5. What is something you are facing that you can't handle without help from your spouse?

6. Reread the passages from question 5 on page 16. How would your marriage improve if you showed more of this kind of love?

7. Look again at the passages about the purpose to which God calls us to in life (question 11 on page 19). What types of things can keep you from pursuing these goals in your life?

8. Rate yourself on a scale of 1 (low) to 10 (high) on how you have been doing during the past week in demonstrating Christ-like love toward your spouse. How can you improve your score this week?

Interact as a Couple [30 minutes]

1. Discuss your answers to questions 1-7 in the previous section.

2. Discuss further one task you agree you can't accomplish alone. How can you work together to accomplish this?

3. Read Matthew 7:24-27. How does working together help build a solid foundation in your marriage?

4. Close your time in prayer. Ask God to help you as you seek to work together as a team.

Remember to bring your calendar to the next session to Make a Date.

Equal, Yet Different

While God has created men and women with unique
differences, both have equal worth in Christ.

W A R M • U P   15   M I N U T E S

"One Thing I've Learned..."

By completing one of the following statements, tell
about something you have learned from marriage
(remember, don't share anything that would embarrass your spouse):

- One thing marriage has taught me about the
  opposite sex is...

- One assumption that I had going into marriage
  that I quickly discovered was mistaken was...

- One thing I've learned about relating to one's
  spouse is that, whenever possible, you should...

After everyone has completed a sentence, discuss this
question: How can these lessons be used to help
build teamwork in marriage?

Project Report

Share one thing you learned from last session's HomeBuilders Project.

BLUEPRINTS   60 MINUTES

It's not hard to recognize there are differences between men and women. But beyond the obvious physical differences, men and women are different from one another in a variety of ways. However, recognizing these differences is one thing, while appreciating these differences is quite another!

A Call to Understanding

If you have a large group, form smaller groups of about six people to answer the Blueprints questions. Unless otherwise noted, answer the questions in your subgroup. After finishing each section, take time for subgroups to share their answers with the whole group.

In Genesis 1:27 we read, "So God created man in his own image, in the image of God he created him; male and female he created them." When God created the human race, he divided humanity into "male and female," and called them "very good."

1. From your observation, what are some common, nonphysical ways that men and women are different?

2. Read 1 Peter 3:7. Why do you think husbands are called to be considerate, or understanding, in relation to their wives? If this exhortation had been addressed to wives, how might it have been stated differently?

3. Practically, what are some ways a husband and wife can gain a better understanding of each other?

4. Why is it important for a husband and wife to understand the differences between men and women?

5. When has such an understanding helped you in your marriage?

Equal Worth

6. Read 1 Peter 3:7 again. How is this verse a reflection of how husbands and wives are different and equal?

7. What additional insight do you find in Galatians 3:26-29 about how all people are equal before God?

8. What do you think it means, practically, to be "one in Christ Jesus"? What effect should being one in Christ have on how we relate to other Christians? on how you relate to your spouse?

9. What can happen in a marriage when one spouse does not regard the other as having equal worth before God?

Different Functions

10. Read 1 Corinthians 12:12-26. In what ways is marriage like a body: "a unit...made up of many parts"?

11. What is an important, but perhaps under-appreciated, task or function your spouse provides in your marriage? Thank your spouse for performing this task or function.

Answer questions 11 and 12 with your spouse. After answering, you may want to share an appropriate insight or discovery with the group.

12. Read Matthew 19:4-6. What is one thing you can do to help your marriage place less emphasis on individual rights and more value on teamwork?

W R A P • U P   15   M I N U T E S

As a couple, write two or three ways in which your differences make you stronger as a team (be specific). Then share one of your ideas with the group.

Make a Date

Make a date with your spouse to meet before the next session to complete the HomeBuilders Project. At the next session, your leader will ask for you to share one aspect of this experience.

_____
DATE

_____
TIME

_____
LOCATION

As a Couple [10 minutes]

Start your date by coming up with some examples of great combinations—two things (or people) that are better together than apart. For example, peanut butter and jelly make a great combination.

After you have identified some great combinations, discuss these questions:

- What are the characteristics of a great combination?
- How do these characteristics apply—or not apply—to a marriage?

Individually [20 minutes]

1. What insight, discovery, or reminder from this session did you find most helpful?

2. What is one of the differences between you and your spouse that you've grown to appreciate during your marriage?

3. What is one function your spouse provides for you that you largely take for granted? What is one way you can honor him or her this week for that function?

4. List one or two things you would like your spouse to understand about you—things you feel he or she is unaware of because of your gender difference.

5. List at least one area in which you are having difficulty understanding your spouse.

6. In what ways do you think the things you just listed affect the quality of your marriage? How can you communicate these things in a kind and loving way?

7. What does it mean to you that you and your spouse can have different functions in marriage but still have equal worth in the eyes of God?

Interact as a Couple [30 minutes]

1. Read together Colossians 3:12-17 to set the tone for your discussion.

2. Share with your spouse your answers to the individual questions.

3. Discuss some specific actions you can take as a couple to help promote better understanding between you.

4. Pray, thanking God for each other and for your differences.

Remember to bring your calendar to the next session to Make a Date.

Following Christ's Example

To rightly relate to one another as husband and wife, we need to follow Christ's example of serving others.

W A R M • U P   15   M I N U T E S

Leader or Servant?

In two groups, review the list of personal characteristics that follows. One group should circle five traits from the list they feel are most important for a leader. The other group should select five characteristics that are most important for a servant.

honest	humble	articulate
intelligent	compassionate	persuasive
diplomatic	innovative	optimistic
loving	dependable	loyal
risk-taker	extroverted	likeable
self-confident	outspoken	goal-oriented
flexible	decisive	courageous
motivated	patient	forgiving

After both groups have made their selections, relate which words were picked and discuss the following questions:

- What are some reasons your group picked the words that it did?
- Would you classify the two lists as very similar or very different? Why?
- How are leading and serving different? similar?

Project Report

Share one thing you learned from last session's HomeBuilders Project.

BLUEPRINTS   60 MINUTES

In the first two sessions, we looked at working together as a team and at understanding, appreciating, and honoring each other's differences. In this session, we will examine another foundational teamwork principle. We find this principle illustrated by some surprising actions and words from Jesus.

Called to Serve

"For even the Son of Man did not come to be served, but to serve, and to give his life as a ransom for many" (Mark 10:45).

1. Read John 13:1-17. What was Jesus trying to teach the disciples?

If you have a large group, form smaller groups of about six people to answer the Blueprints questions. Unless otherwise noted, answer the questions in your subgroup. After finishing each section, take time for subgroups to share their answers with the whole group.

2. Why do you think Peter was so resistant to Jesus' actions?

3. How would you describe Jesus' style of leadership? How is footwashing illustrative of how Jesus led?

4. When has someone served you in a way that surprised you? What was your reaction?

5. Read Mark 9:33-35 and Matthew 20:25-28. In what way is Christ's description of a leader different from the way today's world describes a leader?

6. What are some ways that Christ's example of servanthood can be practiced in marriage?

Called to Humility

7. Read Philippians 2:1-8, in which Paul expounds on the theme of servanthood. How do the actions described in Philippians 2:1-8 reflect the kind of servanthood Jesus modeled?

8. What happens in marriage when you look only to your own self-interests?

9. What are some ways in your marriage that you can better practice Christ's example of servanthood?

Answer questions 9 and 10 with your spouse. After answering, you may want to share an appropriate insight or discovery with the group.

10. When has your spouse recently displayed the attitude discussed in Philippians 2—showing humility and not acting from selfish ambition or vain conceit?

Meeting Needs

Part of serving your spouse is making a commitment to meet one another's needs.

11. Everyone has needs, but some needs are of greater importance to women than they are to men—and vice versa.

Women: Share what you believe are some special needs that women have in their marriages. Men, listen carefully, and take notes!

Men: Share what you believe are some special needs that men have in their marriages. Women, listen carefully, and take notes!

12. Read Ephesians 5:33. What are husbands told to do? What are wives told to do? What are some practical ways that you can demonstrate these respective attitudes toward your spouse?

HomeBuilders Principle:
In life and in marriage, Christ calls us to a radical concept—to serve others rather than ourselves.

W R A P • U P   15   M I N U T E S

In groups of men and women, brainstorm lists of ways that you can serve your spouse. After your group has come up with several ideas, select an idea that you will do this week, and tell your group. (*Don't* tell your spouse what you're planning to do—let it be a surprise!)

Make a Date

Make a date with your spouse to meet before the next session to complete the HomeBuilders Project. At the next session, your leader will ask for you to share one aspect of this experience.

DATE

TIME

LOCATION

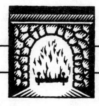

HOMEBUILDERS PROJECT   6 0   M I N U T E S

As a Couple [10 minutes]

Revisit the list of personal characteristics on page 35. Select two or three words that you believe are reflective of your spouse. Then share with your spouse the words you selected and why you selected them.

Individually [20 minutes]

The importance of maintaining an attitude of servant-hood in marriage can become more apparent as you think of how your lives will change as you grow older. Using the chart on the following page, think about the issues you will face individually and as a couple in the future. For example: What financial pressures do you think you will face? What will be your daily schedule? What will be the likely state of your health? What career pressures or decisions will you make? If you have children or plan to have children, be sure to factor this into your discussion as well. Think of what ages your children will be and how the presence of children will affect you as a couple.

During this individual time, record the issues you think you may be facing individually and as a couple in the years to come. Then, when you come back together, you will compare charts and work on the last column.

	Issues we'll face individually	Issues we'll face as a couple	Ways we'll need to serve each other
Next 1-2 years			
5 years from now			
10 years from now			
More than 20 years from now			

Interact as a Couple [30 minutes]

1. Share your charts with each other.

2. Discuss and record ways you can serve each other.

3. Close in prayer. Ask God for wisdom and help in serving each other.

Remember to bring your calendar to the next session to Make a Date.

Biblical Responsibilities

The Bible sets forth key responsibilities for
husbands and wives.

W A R M • U P   15   M I N U T E S

Who Does What?

During the next few minutes, write down a list of the
household tasks for which you and your spouse take
responsibility on a regular basis. For example, if you
typically mow the lawn and your spouse feeds the
dog, list those tasks under the appropriate column on
the following chart.

Husband	Wife

After compiling your lists, answer the following questions:

- What process, if any, did you go through as a couple to decide who would do what?
- What would happen in your marriage if you didn't have any set tasks or chores and you negotiated each day about who would do what?

Project Report

Share one thing you learned from last session's HomeBuilders Project.

BLUEPRINTS   60 MINUTES

There is often great misunderstanding concerning what the Bible says about the different functions and responsibilities a husband and wife should assume in a marriage. Therefore it is extremely important that you don't jump to conclusions about what this session will teach. The responsibilities for husbands and wives should not be viewed as comprehensive lifestyles. In other words, while these responsibilities are important, they do not cover all that one does. There is great latitude, creativity, and flexibility around one's responsibilities in marriage.

An Overall Perspective

In time, every marriage settles into some social and organizational arrangement. Both husband and wife assume specific responsibilities that uphold the arrangement.

In Ephesians 5:21, Paul instructs us to "submit to one another out of reverence for Christ." This instruction echoes the passages we studied in the last session, when we learned about our call to humility and servanthood. But Paul doesn't stop there. In the remainder of the chapter, he describes how this "submission" looks for different people.

1. In two groups of roughly equal size, read Ephesians 5:22-33. Then answer the following questions:

- As a husband or a wife, what strikes you about this passage?

- How relevant do you believe the passage's instructions to husbands and wives are today?

After each group has answered these questions, gather together and compare answers.

A Husband's Key Responsibilities

If you have a large group, form smaller groups of about six people to answer the Blueprints questions. Unless otherwise noted, answer the questions in your subgroup. After finishing each section, take time for subgroups to share their answers with the whole group.

2. Reread Ephesians 5:22-27. What is your present understanding of Paul's statement, "For the husband is the head of the wife"?

3. What dangers or misunderstandings are possible with the concept of "headship"?

4. Notice again Ephesians 5:23. With whom is the husband's leadership style to be compared? In light of what we studied about servanthood in the last session, what does this mean to you?

5. In the last session we looked at how Jesus led. Read Luke 22:25-27. What styles of leadership does Jesus contrast? Against which of these styles do people react? Why?

6. Look again at Ephesians 5:25-27, and Ephesians 5:31-32. What do you think it means for a husband to love his wife "just as Christ loved the church and gave himself up for her"? How might this kind of love look in a marriage relationship?

A Wife's Key Responsibilities

7. Read Genesis 2:18-22. What words or images come to mind when you think of a wife as a husband's "helper"?

8. Read how God is described in Psalm 10:14, Psalm 118:7, and Isaiah 41:10, 13-14. Considering these verses, how do you think God views the role of "helper"?

———

9. Read Proverbs 31:10-31 and Titus 2:3-5. What perspectives do these passages add to your understanding of a wife's responsibilities?

10. What do you think is meant by the words "to be busy at home" in Titus 2:5, as related to a wife's responsibilities?

11. Proverbs 31 describes the wife as engaged both in business (verses 16 and 18) and in looking after her household (verse 27). Which of these undertakings do you believe is most reflective of a wife's responsibilities? Why?

Making Application

Work on item 12 individually, then share your response with your spouse.

12. Look back at the Bible passages we've reviewed in this session. Underline the key words that help define our responsibilities in marriage. Then write down what you see as your key responsibilities as a husband or wife.

HomeBuilders Principle:
Husbands and wives each have unique God-appointed responsibilities to fulfill in marriage.

W R A P • U P   15 M I N U T E S

Any discussion about biblical responsibilities in marriage can lead to sharp disagreements. Many people bring to the debate their own views shaped by experience, by their childhoods, and by how their

Each person should select one of the statements that follow to respond to. Discuss with your spouse your response, and then share it with the group.

philosophies have been shaped by the world we live in. From what we've learned about how God views teamwork in marriage, how might you respond to one of the following statements:

Ward: *I think all marriages should be the way it was when I was growing up—you know, "traditional." The man should bring home the bacon, and the woman should fry it up in the pan.*

Gloria: *Essentially, the institution of marriage exists to oppress women. I mean, a woman gets married and is supposed to change her name? It's like you're not your own person anymore. A woman is equal to a man and shouldn't lower herself to the subjection of marriage.*

Gilbert: *Marriage should be an equal partnership. The only specific responsibilities a husband or wife should assume are ones that have been mutually agreed upon, based on each other's gifts and abilities.*

Make a Date

Make a date with your spouse to meet before the next session to complete the HomeBuilders Project. At the next session, your leader will ask for you to share one aspect of this experience.

DATE

TIME

LOCATION

HOMEBUILDERS PROJECT   6 0   M I N U T E S

As a Couple [10 minutes]

If you could assume the role of anyone—real or fictional—for a day, who would it be? What is it about the person's life that appeals to you?

Individually [20 minutes]

1. Looking back over this session, what is one idea you can apply to be a better teammate in your marriage?

2. Review the following list of "voices" that influence us in how we determine our responsibilities in marriage. Which have influenced you the most in how your marriage is currently structured? Rank them 1-6, using 1 to represent the most influential and 6 as the least influential.

___ how I saw my parents live out their marriage

___ what I have absorbed from the culture

___ how my peers have structured their marriages

___ what I understand the Bible to teach about marriage

___ what I have studied, read in books, or learned in school

___ other:

3. Up to this point, what would you say your vision of your key responsibilities in marriage has been? In what way, if any, has this changed?

4. Read the designated scenarios and respond to the questions that follow.

For Husbands:

Chuck is an old-school, take-charge kind of guy. In his office hangs a poster with a saying that serves as his motto: "Lead, follow, or get out of the way." Chuck is results-oriented and is accustomed to getting things done his way. For the most part, his aggressive style of leadership has served him well in the business world. But at home, well, that's a different story. Chuck expects the same lock step obedience from his wife and kids that he gets from his subordinates at work. This expectation has caused ongoing tension between him and his wife. When his wife disagrees with him, he often tells her, "The Good Book says I'm the head of this house."

When Ron and Becky were married, they determined they would have a "50/50 marriage." They would divide their household tasks evenly, they would share equally in raising their children, they would make all decisions together. Now that they've been married six years, Ron wonders whether this arrangement is working. They often have big arguments over whether they truly meet each other halfway. Sometimes, Ron thinks, it's easier just to let Becky have her own way, rather than risk another big blowup.

- Of the examples of Chuck and Ron, who can you relate to most? Why?

- In what ways do Chuck and Ron need to change?

- What is the biggest challenge you face in fulfilling your biblical responsibilities as a husband?

- What is one step you can take to better fulfill your biblical responsibilities as a husband?

For Wives:

Karla is thirty-four and has been married four years. Her husband, Blair, is a successful stockbroker, and she is happy and fulfilled in her work as a marketing consultant. She and her husband are thinking of beginning a family, but she is hesitant because of the impact it would have on her career.

Maria thinks she understands what the Bible says about a wife being a "helper" in a marriage, but it doesn't seem fair to her. "Why should the husband be the 'leader,' just because he's a man?" she asks. "There are some things I can do better. For one thing, I'm better at handling our finances. Am I not as important to God because I'm a woman?"

- Which of these women, Karla or Maria, can you most relate to? Why?

- How would you advise these women in relation to their biblical responsibilities?

- What is the biggest challenge you face in fulfilling your biblical responsibilities as a wife?

- What is one step you can take to better fulfill your biblical responsibilities as a wife?

Interact as a Couple [30 minutes]

1. Discuss your answers from the previous section.

2. The first three sessions of this study introduced four foundational principles for building teamwork in marriage:

- We are to show Christ-like love to each other.
- We are to pursue biblical goals together.
- In any team, people can assume different functions yet still have equal worth.
- Christ calls us to radical servanthood in our marriage relationship.

Based on what you have studied in this session, discuss why these biblical principles are important to remember when you look at the differing responsibilities of a husband and a wife.

3. Read Psalm 127:1. Discuss how this verse relates to the structure of your marriage.

4. Pray, asking God to help you understand and fulfill your God-given responsibilities as husband and wife.

Remember to bring your calendar to the next session to Make a Date.

Biblical Responses

A husband and wife can help each other fulfill their biblical responsibilities by how they respond to one another.

W A R M • U P   15   M I N U T E S

Likely Responses

Working individually, select the response that you believe your spouse would most likely have in each of the following situations. Mark that response with an S. Then, select the response that you would most likely have, and mark it with an M.

1. The family dog has just tracked mud across the newly cleaned carpet. Likely first response:

___ get really mad at the dog

___ laugh

___ cry

___ launch an immediate and intense investigation into how this happened and who is responsible

(choices continued on next page)

___ get mad at someone in the family for allowing this to happen

___ clean up the mess

2. Your spouse has just defeated you in a friendly game of tennis. Likely first response:

___ congratulate the winner on his or her skill and prowess

___ demand a rematch

___ suddenly grow unusually quiet and moody

___ complain about a sore elbow

___ silently vow revenge and patiently wait for just the right opportunity

After marking your responses, get with your spouse and compare results. Then discuss these questions as a group:

- How well did you predict your spouse's responses?
- When you find yourself in a situation like one of the previous scenarios, how much does your anticipation of your spouse's response affect you?
- What effect can the "right" response from your spouse have on you?

Project Report

Share one thing you learned from last session's HomeBuilders Project.

BLUEPRINTS   6o MINUTES

A Wife's Response

Many Christians believe a husband's responsibility is to be the head of his family and a wife's responsibility is to submit to her husband. However, submission may more appropriately be seen as a *response* rather than a responsibility.

If you have a large group, form smaller groups of about six people to answer the Blueprints questions. Unless otherwise noted, answer the questions in your subgroup. After finishing each section, take time for subgroups to share their answers with the whole group.

1. Read the following verses:

- Ephesians 5:21-24
- Colossians 3:18
- 1 Peter 3:1-6

What do you think it means to submit or be submissive? What kind of emotions does the concept of submission raise?

2. Why do you think the Scripture mentions the church's submission to Christ as a model for a wife's submission to her husband?

3. Why do you think Bible passages that refer to husbands and wives never tell the husband to make his wife submit?

4. What are some of the hang-ups people have regarding the concept of "submission"? Under what circumstances should a wife not submit to her husband? Why?

5. If a husband is fulfilling his biblical responsibilities, what effect do you think this fulfillment would have on his wife's attitude about submission?

6. How do you think submission can be demonstrated in marriage?

A Husband's Response

Just as the Scripture calls for a wife to respond to her husband's responsibilities, it also requires a husband to respond to his wife's responsibilities.

7. An often-neglected aspect of a husband's call to love his wife is how that love is demonstrated. Read the following Scriptures:

- Ephesians 5:28-29
- Colossians 3:19
- 1 Peter 3:7

In these verses, what key words or admonishments describe the kind of response a wife needs from her husband?

8. Read Proverbs 31:28-31. From these verses, what is the husband's response to his wife? Do you think his attitude is the cause or result of her actions? Why?

9. Why is a husband's praise important to a wife's success in fulfilling her biblical responsibilities?

10. What could be the results in a marriage in which a wife does not receive encouragement or praise from her husband?

11. What are some practical ways these responsibilities can be demonstrated in marriage?

Making Application

Work on item 12 individually, then share your answer with your spouse.

12. Look back at the Bible passages we've reviewed in this session. Underline the key words that help define what our biblical response to our spouse should be. Then write down what your response or attitude should be in support of your spouse fulfilling his or her biblical responsibilities. Also, write one way you can put your response into practice during the next week.

HomeBuilders Principle:
Husbands and wives are called to respond to each other in ways that will help them fulfill their God-appointed responsibilities.

W R A P • U P   15 M I N U T E S

As a couple, discuss a challenge—big or small—that you are facing. Talk about how you can biblically respond to one another in a supportive and encouraging way as you deal with this issue.

Conclude by praying with your spouse. Pray for each other and about the challenge you just discussed.

Make a Date

Make a date with your spouse to meet before the next session to complete the HomeBuilders Project. At the next session, your leader will ask for you to share one aspect of this experience.

DATE

_____

TIME

_____

LOCATION

HOMEBUILDERS PROJECT   6 0   M I N U T E S

As a Couple [10 minutes]

Start your date by responding to one of the following questions:

- From a movie, song, TV show, or real life, what is a response you have heard or observed that impressed you and made you think, "Wow, that was a *great* response. If I'm ever in that situation, I hope I can respond like that"?
- When is a time your spouse has really impressed you with a response to you or to another person?

Individually [20 minutes]

1. Having studied and discussed responsibilities and responses in marriage during the past two sessions, what is one way you have been challenged?

2. Up to this point in your marriage, what grade would you give yourself for supporting your spouse in his or her responsibilities in marriage? Explain.

3. Think about how you have responded to your spouse during the past week. What grade would you give yourself? Why?

4. What is one change you could make to better support your spouse and improve your grade?

5. What is one practical way your spouse could help you fulfill your responsibilities as a husband or wife?

6. In your marriage, what is an example of something your spouse has done—an action or perhaps timely words—that really encouraged you?

7. In having studied and discussed responsibilities and responses in marriage, you may have confronted attitudes and actions for which you are sorry. Spend a few minutes in prayer. Confess to God your attitudes and actions.

Interact as a Couple [30 minutes]

1. Discuss your answers to questions 1-6 of the previous section.

2. Read Proverbs 31:10-31 and discuss the following:

- How would you characterize the relationship between the husband and wife in this passage?

- In what way is the relationship that the passage descibes like or unlike your relationship?

- Which traits would you like to see reflected more in your relationship? How can you accomplish this?

3. If you have come to recognize shortcomings in the way you have handled your responsibilities in your marriage or your response to your spouse's responsibilities, apologize to each other, doing so in a humble and loving way.

4. Close in prayer, praying that God will help you as you seek to properly respond to and support each other.

Remember to bring your calendar to the next session to Make a Date.

Making Teamwork Work

Through the power of the Holy Spirit, you can apply
the principles of teamwork in your marriage.

W A R M • U P   15   M I N U T E S

Checking In

Complete one, or both, of the following phrases:

This course has helped our teamwork in marriage by…

One thing I want to change in myself as a result of
this study is…

Project Report

Share one thing you learned from last session's
HomeBuilders Project.

Having discussed biblical responsibilities and responses for husbands and wives, let's see how these concepts might apply to everyday living.

Responsibilities, Responses, and the *Real* World

Following are four case studies. Divide into two groups, with each group looking at two stories. Read your stories and discuss the questions. Then report to the other group, summarizing the scenarios you examined and your discussion about what should be done.

1. Barney and Betty are expecting their first child. Both Barney and Betty agree that it would be ideal if Betty could quit her job and become a stay-at-home mother. However, they are concerned about whether they could make ends meet, as they depend on her income.

- What do you think Barney and Betty should do?

- In what way do biblical responsibilities and responses play into this scenario?

2. Raymond is the type of man who is not afraid to say what he thinks. Often this trait is an asset, but it also leads him into conflict on a regular basis. For example, his wife, Sherry, doesn't like going out to eat at a nice restaurant because she knows that Raymond will probably antagonize the waiter by making critical comments and unrealistic demands.

This year their oldest son began playing on a Little League baseball team, and it didn't take long for Raymond to find conflict in this new arena. He argues with coaches about their strategies or about the amount of playing time his son gets.

Whenever Sherry tries to talk to Raymond about his behavior, he becomes angry. When she asks friends at church what she should do, some urge her to boldly confront her husband, while others counsel her just to pray because "it's not right for you to tell him what he's doing wrong—he's the head of the home and you're supposed to submit to him."

- What do you think Sherry should do?

- In what way do biblical responsibilities and responses play into this scenario?

3. Early in their marriage, Jack and Diane took a personality test that confirmed their suspicion. Jack is a quiet, precise, reflective type who does not take to leadership naturally. Diane is just the opposite— an aggressive, articulate, people-oriented woman who seems to rise to leadership positions easily.

As they contemplate their biblical responsibilities, they feel some conflict. For years Diane has assumed the dominant leadership role in their home, while Jack has grown increasingly passive. Diane wants to see Jack take more leadership in their home, but at the same time she doesn't want to become a wallflower. Jack, meanwhile, isn't confident of his ability to lead.

- What do you think Jack and Diane should do?

- In what way do biblical responsibilities and responses play into this scenario?

4. Lee and Susan have been married eight years and have three children, ages 1, 3, and 5. Lee provides for the family's needs through his work as a corporate lawyer, and Susan is a full-time mother.

Their problems begin when Lee arrives home. He is tired from a busy day at work and wants to relax in his favorite chair in front of the television for awhile. Susan, meanwhile, finds it difficult to prepare their dinner while also supervising the kids. Lee plays with the children each night after dinner, but just about the time they need to get ready for bed, he usually goes into his den and either makes some work-related phone calls or completes some paperwork.

Susan is tired of this routine, and Lee is tired of her complaining. "I'm doing my job, and you're doing yours," he says.

- What do you think should happen in Lee and Susan's relationship?

- In what way do biblical responsibilities and responses play into this scenario?

Answer questions 5 and 6 with your spouse. After answering, you may want to share an appropriate insight or discovery with the group.

5. Thinking back over your marriage, what is one situation you might handle differently now, based on your current understanding of biblical responsibilities in marriage?

6. When you think about what you have discussed in this course about building teamwork in marriage, what seems to be the most difficult thing for you to apply?

Succeeding in the Spirit

If you have a large group, form smaller groups of about six people to answer the Blueprints questions. Unless otherwise noted, answer the questions in your subgroup. After finishing each section, take time for subgroups to share their answers with the whole group.

When you look at what God says about marriage, it's easy to feel overwhelmed. And that's why God offers help to us.

7. Read John 14:15-26. What promise does Jesus make to his followers? What insights do these verses give about the Holy Spirit?

8. What are some ways that help from the Holy Spirit could be experienced in marriage?

Hindering the Holy Spirit

Within all of us is a natural inclination to go our own way, to reject God's direction and resist God's help. This streak of independence, which found its way into the heart of humanity when Adam and Eve first disobeyed God, has passed along to all subsequent generations.

9. Read the following passages:

- Romans 7:18-21
- Romans 8:5-8
- Galatians 5:19-21a

What do these verses say about our natural inclination, our "sinful nature"?

10. Of the various ways the sinful nature influences us, which do you feel is most harmful to teamwork in marriage? Why?

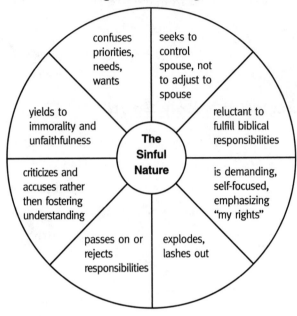

Ways the Sinful Nature Works Against a Marriage

- confuses priorities, needs, wants
- seeks to control spouse, not to adjust to spouse
- yields to immorality and unfaithfulness
- reluctant to fulfill biblical responsibilities
- The Sinful Nature
- criticizes and accuses rather then fostering understanding
- is demanding, self-focused, emphasizing "my rights"
- passes on or rejects responsibilities
- explodes, lashes out

Defeating Selfishness

God has placed the Holy Spirit within every Christian so that our sinful nature can be opposed and resisted. Having two opposing forces vying for our obedience creates an ongoing internal conflict which most of us feel every day.

11. Read the following passages:

- Romans 6:12-14
- Romans 8:5-8
- Romans 12:1-2
- Galatians 5:16-18

What do these verses say about our choices in this battle?

12. Refer to the diagram showing the benefits of the Holy Spirit in marriage. Which of these benefits could you use the most right now in your life or marriage?

Ways the Holy Spirit Works in a Marriage

The Holy Spirit

- promotes the priority of raising God-honoring children
- seeks the best for both husband and wife
- clarifies priorities and needs from impulsive wants
- encourages forgiveness and understanding between a couple
- recalls what God's Word says in crucial moments of a marriage
- convicts of selfishness, thoughts or acts of impurity, immorality, and outbursts of anger
- helps one to fulfill biblical responsibilities
- guides according to the will of God

HomeBuilders Principle:
The Holy Spirit can equip you to fulfill what God desires for you in marriage.

As you reach the end of this course, take a few minutes to reflect on your experience. Review the following questions, and write responses to the questions you can answer. Then relate to the group one or more of your answers.

- What has this group meant to you during the course of this study? Be specific.

- What is the most valuable lesson that you have learned or discovered?

- How has this study changed or challenged you or your marriage?

- What would you like to see happen next for this group?

Make a Date

Make a date with your spouse to meet this week to complete the last HomeBuilders Project of this study.

_____
DATE

_____
TIME

_____
LOCATION

HOMEBUILDERS PROJECT   6 0   M I N U T E S

As a Couple [10 minutes]

Part of building teamwork in your marriage is making an ongoing commitment to know and understand each other better. One way to do this is to date your spouse. Start this date by planning another date—a date without homework! To plan your date, consider the following:

- What would you like to do? Visit a museum? Go

out to dinner and a show? Take a romantic overnight trip? Pick something you both would like to do. Decide which of you will make necessary arrangements (such as making reservations).

- When can you go on your date? Look at your calendars and schedule your outing.
- If you have kids, discuss child-care arrangements for your date. Decide who will make the arrangements for child care.

Individually [20 minutes]

1. During the first meeting of this study, what expectations did you have for this course? How did your experience compare to your expectations?

2. What has been the best part of this study for you?

3. How have the principles you've studied in this course helped you build teamwork in your marriage?

4. Looking back, what action do you need to follow up on?

5. Where in your life or marriage do you most need to experience the power of the Holy Spirit right now?

6. What might be hindering the Holy Spirit's work in your life?

7. Pray, and confess to God any sin that is hindering the Holy Spirit's work in your life. Ask God to help you walk in the Spirit (you may also want to read "Part Two: Living the Christian Life," which starts on page 95).

Interact as a Couple [30 minutes]

1. Discuss your answers from the previous individual section.

2. Evaluate some things you might do to continue building teamwork in your marriage, building up each other, and building up other people. For example, consider regularly setting aside time together, as you have for these HomeBuilder Projects. You may also want to consider some ideas from page 87 in "Where Do You Go From Here?"

3. Pray, asking the Lord for help through the Holy Spirit as you seek to continue the process of building teamwork in your marriage.

Please visit our Web site at www.familylife.com/homebuilders to give us your feedback on this study and to get information about other FamilyLife resources and conferences.

Where Do You Go From Here?

●

It is our prayer that you have benefited greatly from this study in the HomeBuilders Couples Series. We hope that your marriage will continue to grow as you both submit your lives to Jesus Christ and build according to his blueprints.

We also hope that you will begin reaching out to strengthen other marriages in your community and local church. Your church needs couples like you who are committed to building Christian marriages. A favorite World War II story illustrates this point very clearly.

The year was 1940. The French Army had just collapsed under Hitler's onslaught. The Dutch had folded, overwhelmed by the Nazi regime. The Belgians had surrendered. And the British Army was trapped on the coast of France in the channel port of Dunkirk.

Two hundred and twenty thousand of Britain's finest young men seemed doomed to die, turning the English Channel red with their blood. The Fuehrer's troops, only miles away in the hills of France, didn't realize how close to victory they actually were.

Any rescue seemed feeble and futile in the time remaining. A "thin" British Navy—"the professionals"—told King George VI that at best they could save 17,000 troops. The House of Commons was warned to prepare for "hard and heavy tidings."

Politicians were paralyzed. The king was powerless. And the Allies could only watch as spectators from a distance. Then as the doom of the British Army seemed imminent, a strange fleet appeared on the horizon of the English Channel—the wildest assortment of boats perhaps ever assembled in history.

Trawlers, tugs, scows, fishing sloops, lifeboats, pleasure craft, smacks and coasters, sailboats, even the London fire-brigade flotilla. *Each ship was manned by civilian volunteers—English fathers sailing to rescue Britain's exhausted, bleeding sons.*

William Manchester writes in his epic book, *The Last Lion*, that even today what happened in 1940 in less than twenty-four hours seems like a miracle—not only were all of the British soldiers rescued, but 118,000 other Allied troops as well.

Today the Christian home is much like those troops at Dunkirk. Pressured, trapped, and demoralized, it needs help. Your help. The Christian community may be much like England—we stand waiting for politicians, professionals, even for our pastors to step in and save the family. But the problem is much larger than all of those combined can solve.

With the highest divorce rate of any nation on earth, we need an all-out effort by men and women "sailing" to rescue the exhausted and wounded family casualties. We need an outreach effort by common couples with faith in an uncommon God. For too long, married couples within the church have abdicated the privilege and responsibility of influencing others to those in full-time vocational ministry.

Possibly this study has indeed been used to "light the torch" of your spiritual lives. Perhaps it was already burning, and this provided more fuel. Regardless, may we challenge you to invest your lives in others?

You and other couples around the world can team together to build thousands of marriages and families. By starting a HomeBuilders group, you will not only strengthen other marriages but you will also see your marriage grow as you share these principles with others.

Will You Join Us in "Touching Lives...Changing Families"?

The following are some practical ways you can make a difference in families today:

1. Gather a group of four to eight couples, and lead them through the six sessions of this HomeBuilders study, *Building Teamwork in Your Marriage.* (Why not consider challenging others in your church or community to form additional HomeBuilders groups?)

2. Commit to continue marriage building by doing another course in the HomeBuilders Couples Series.

3. An excellent outreach tool is the film *"JESUS,"* which is available on video. For more information, contact FamilyLife at 1-800-FL-TODAY.

4. Host a dinner party. Invite families from your neighborhood to your home, and as a couple share your faith in Christ.

5. Reach out and share the love of Christ with neighborhood children.

6. If you have attended the FamilyLife Marriage Conference, why not offer to assist your pastor in counseling couples engaged to be married, using the material you received?

For more information about any of the above ministry opportunities, contact your local church, or write:

> **FamilyLife**
> P.O. Box 8220
> Little Rock, AR 72221-8220
> 1-800-FL-TODAY
> **www.familylife.com**

Our Problems, God's Answers

Every couple eventually has to deal with problems in marriage. Communication problems. Money problems. Difficulties with sexual intimacy. These issues are important to cultivating a strong, loving relationship with your spouse. The HomeBuilders Couples Series is designed to help you strengthen your marriage in many of these critical areas.

Part One: The Big Problem

One basic problem is at the heart of every other problem in every marriage, and it's a problem we can't help you fix. No matter how hard you try, this is one problem that is too big for you to deal with on your own.

The problem is separation from God. If you want to experience marriage the way it was designed to be, you need a vital relationship with the God who created you and offers you the power to live a life of joy and purpose.

And what separates us from God is one more problem—sin. Most of us have assumed throughout our lives that the term "sin" refers to a list of bad habits that everyone agrees are wrong. We try to deal with our sin problem by working hard to become better people. We read books to learn how to control our anger, or we resolve to stop cheating on our taxes.

But in our hearts, we know our sin problem runs much deeper than a list of bad habits. All of us have rebelled against God. We have ignored him and have decided to run our own lives in a way that makes sense to us. The Bible says that the God who created us wants us to follow his plan for our lives. But because of our sin problem, we think our ideas and plans are better than his.

- *"For all have sinned and fall short of the glory of God"* (Romans 3:23).

What does it mean to "fall short of the glory of God"? It means that none of us has trusted and treasured God the way we should. We have sought to satisfy ourselves with other things and have treated those things as more valuable than God. We have gone our own way. According to the Bible, we have to pay a penalty for our sin. We cannot simply do things the way we choose and hope it will all be OK with God. Following our own plan leads to our destruction.

- *"There is a way that seems right to a man, but in the end it leads to death"* (Proverbs 14:12).

- *"For the wages of sin is death"* (Romans 6:23a).

The penalty for sin is that we are forever separated from God's love. God is holy, and we are sinful. No matter how hard we try, we cannot come up with some plan, like living a good life or even trying to do what the Bible says, and hope that we can avoid the penalty.

God's Solution to Sin

Thankfully, God has a way to solve our dilemma. He became a man through the person of Jesus Christ. He lived a holy life, in perfect obedience to God's plan. He also willingly died on a cross to pay our penalty for sin. Then he proved that he is more powerful than sin or death by rising from the dead. He alone has the power to overrule the penalty for our sin.

- *"Jesus answered, 'I am the way and the truth and the life. No one comes to the Father except through me' "* (John 14:6).

- *"But God demonstrates his own love for us in this: While we were still sinners, Christ died for us"* (Romans 5:8).

- *"Christ died for our sins...he was buried...he was raised on the third day according to the Scriptures...he appeared to Peter, and then to the Twelve. After that, he appeared to more than five hundred"* (1 Corinthians 15:3-6).

- *"For the wages of sin is death, but the gift of God is eternal life in Christ Jesus our Lord"* (Romans 6:23).

The death of Jesus has fixed our sin problem. He has bridged the gap between God and us. He is calling all of us to come to him and to give up our own flawed plan for how to run our lives. He wants us to trust God and his plan.

Accepting God's Solution

If you agree that you are separated from God, he is calling you to confess your sins. All of us have made messes of our lives because we have stubbornly preferred our ideas and plans over his. As a result, we deserve to be cut off from God's love and his care for us. But God has promised that if we will agree that we have rebelled against his plan for us and have messed up our lives, he will forgive us and will fix our sin problem.

- *"Yet to all who received him, to those who believed in his name, he gave the right to become children of God" (John 1:12).*

- *"For it is by grace you have been saved, through faith—and this not from yourselves, it is the gift of*

God—not by works, so that no one can boast" (Ephesians 2:8-9).

When the Bible talks about receiving Christ, it means we acknowledge that we are sinners and that we can't fix the problem ourselves. It means we turn away from our sin. And it means we trust Christ to forgive our sins and to make us the kind of people he wants us to be. It's not enough to just intellectually believe that Christ is the Son of God. We must trust in him and his plan for our lives by faith, as an act of the will.

Are things right between you and God, with him and his plan at the center of your life? Or is life spinning out of control as you seek to make your way on your own?

You can decide today to make a change. You can turn to Christ and allow him to transform your life. All you need to do is to talk to him and tell him what is stirring in your mind and in your heart. If you've never done this before, consider taking the steps listed here:

- Do you agree that you need God? Tell God.

- Have you made a mess of your life by following your own plan? Tell God.

- Do you want God to forgive you? Tell God.

- Do you believe that Jesus' death on the cross and his resurrection from the dead gave him the power to fix your sin problem and to grant you the gift of eternal life? Tell God.

- Are you ready to acknowledge that God's plan for your life is better than any plan you could come up with? Tell God.

- Do you agree that God has the right to be the Lord and master of your life? Tell God.

> *"Seek the Lord while he may be found;*
> *call on him while he is near"*
> (Isaiah 55:6).

Following is a suggested prayer:

Lord Jesus, I need you. Thank you for dying on the cross for my sins. I receive you as my Savior and Lord. Thank you for forgiving my sins and giving me eternal life. Make me the kind of person you want me to be.

Does this prayer express the desire of your heart? If it does, pray it right now, and Christ will come into your life, as he promised.

Part Two: Living the Christian Life

For a person who is a follower of Christ—a Christian—the penalty for sin is paid in full. But the effect of sin continues throughout our lives.

- *"If we claim to be without sin, we deceive ourselves and the truth is not in us"* (1 John 1:8).

- *"For what I do is not the good I want to do; no, the evil I do not want to do—this I keep on doing"* (Romans 7:19).

The effects of sin carry over into our marriages as well. Even Christians struggle to maintain solid, God-honoring marriages. Most couples eventually realize that they can't do it on their own. But with God's help, they can succeed. The Holy Spirit can have a huge impact in the marriages of Christians who live constantly, moment by moment, under his gracious direction.

Self-Centered Christians

Many Christians struggle to live the Christian life in their own strength because they are not allowing God to control their lives. Their interests are self-directed, often resulting in failure and frustration.

- *"Brothers, I could not address you as spiritual but as worldly—mere infants in Christ. I gave you milk, not solid food, for you were not yet ready for it. Indeed, you are still not ready. You are still worldly. For since there is jealousy and quarreling among you, are you not worldly? Are you not acting like mere men?"* (1 Corinthians 3:1-3).

The self-centered Christian cannot experience the abundant and fruitful Christian life. Such people trust in their own efforts to live the Christian life: They are either uninformed about—or have forgotten—God's love, forgiveness, and power. This kind of Christian

- has an up-and-down spiritual experience.

- cannot understand himself—he wants to do what is right, but cannot.

- fails to draw upon the power of the Holy Spirit to live the Christian life.

Some or all of the following traits may characterize the Christian who does not fully trust God:

disobedience	plagued by impure thoughts
lack of love for God and others	jealous
	worrisome
inconsistent prayer life	easily discouraged, frustrated
lack of desire for Bible study	critical
legalistic attitude	lack of purpose

Note: The individual who professes to be a Christian but who continues to practice sin should realize that he may not be a Christian at all, according to Ephesians 5:5 and 1 John 2:3; 3:6, 9.

Spirit-Centered Christians

When a Christian puts Christ on the throne of his life, he yields to God's control. This Christian's interests are directed by the Holy Spirit, resulting in harmony with God's plan.

- *"But the fruit of the Spirit is love, joy, peace, patience, kindness, goodness, faithfulness, gentleness and self-control. Against such things there is no law"* (Galatians 5:22-23).

Jesus said:

- *"I have come that they may have life, and have it to the full"* (John 10:10b).

- *"I am the vine; you are the branches. If a man remains in me and I in him, he will bear much fruit; apart from me you can do nothing"* (John 15:5).

- *"But you will receive power when the Holy Spirit comes on you; and you will be my witnesses in Jerusalem, and in all Judea and Samaria, and to the ends of the earth"* (Acts 1:8).

The following traits result naturally from the Holy Spirit's work in our lives:

Christ centered	love
Holy Spirit empowered	joy
motivated to tell others about Jesus	peace
	patience
dedicated to prayer	kindness
student of God's Word	goodness
trusts God	faithfulness
obeys God	gentleness
	self-control

The degree to which these traits appear in a Christian's life and marriage depends upon the extent to which the Christian trusts the Lord with every detail of life, and upon that person's maturity in Christ. One who is only beginning to understand the ministry of the Holy Spirit should not be discouraged if he is not as fruitful as mature Christians who have known and experienced this truth for a longer period of time.

Giving God Control

Jesus promises his followers an abundant and fruitful life as they allow themselves to be directed and empowered by the Holy Spirit. As we give God control of our lives, Christ lives in and through us in the power of the Holy Spirit (John 15).

If you sincerely desire to be directed and empowered by God, you can turn your life over to the control of the Holy Spirit right now (Matthew 5:6; John 7:37-39).

First, confess your sins to God, agreeing with him that you want to turn from any past sinful patterns in your life. Thank God in faith that he has forgiven all of your sins because Christ died for you (Colossians 2:13-15; 1 John 1:9; 2:1-3; Hebrews 10:1-18).

Be sure to offer every area of your life to God (Romans 12:1-2). Consider what areas you might rather keep to yourself, and be sure you're willing to give God control in those areas.

By faith, commit yourself to living according to the Holy Spirit's guidance and power.

- *Live by the Spirit:* **"So I say, live by the Spirit, and you will not gratify the desires of the sinful nature. For the sinful nature desires what is contrary to the Spirit, and the Spirit what is contrary to the sinful nature. They are in conflict with each other, so that you do not do what you want"** (Galatians 5:16-17).

- *Trust in God's promise:* **"This is the confidence we have in approaching God: that if we ask anything according to his will, he hears us. And if we know that he hears us—whatever we ask—we know that we have what we asked of him"** (1 John 5:14-15).

Expressing Your Faith Through Prayer

Prayer is one way of expressing your faith to God. If the prayer that follows expresses your sincere desire, consider praying the prayer or putting the thoughts into your own words:

> **Dear God, I need you. I acknowledge that I have been directing my own life and that, as a result, I have sinned against you. I thank you that you have forgiven my sins through Christ's death on the cross for me. I now invite Christ to take his place on the throne of my life. Take control of my life through the Holy Spirit as you promised you would if I asked in faith. I now thank you for directing my life and for empowering me through the Holy Spirit.**

Walking in the Spirit

If you become aware of an area of your life (an attitude or an action) that is displeasing to God, simply confess your sin, and thank God that he has forgiven your sins on the basis of Christ's death on the cross. Accept God's love and forgiveness by faith, and continue to have fellowship with him.

If you find that you've taken back control of your life through sin—a definite act of disobedience—try this exercise, "Spiritual Breathing," as you give that control back to God.

1. Exhale. Confess your sin. Agree with God that you've sinned against him, and thank him for his forgiveness of it, according to 1 John 1:9 and Hebrews 10:1-25. Remember that confession involves repentance, a determination to change attitudes and actions.

2. Inhale. Surrender control of your life to Christ, inviting the Holy Spirit to once again take charge. Trust that he now directs and empowers you, according to the command of Galatians 5:16-17 and the promise of 1 John 5:14-15. Returning to your faith in God enables you to continue to experience God's love and forgiveness.

Revolutionizing Your Marriage

This new commitment of your life to God will enrich your marriage. Sharing with your spouse what you've committed to is a powerful step in solidifying this commitment. As you exhibit the Holy Spirit's work within you, your spouse may be drawn to make the same commitment you've made. If both of you have given control of your lives to the Holy Spirit, you'll be able to help each other remain true to God, and your marriage may be revolutionized. With God in charge of your lives, life becomes an amazing adventure.

Leader's Notes

Contents

About Leading a HomeBuilders Group **102**

About the Leader's Notes.......................................**106**

Session One **107**

Session Two...**112**

Session Three **116**

Session Four **119**

Session Five..**124**

Session Six **128**

About Leading a HomeBuilders Group

What is the leader's job?

Your role is that of "facilitator"—one who encourages people to think and to discover what Scripture says, who helps group members feel comfortable, and who keeps things moving forward.

What is the best setting and time schedule for this study?

This study is designed as a small-group home Bible study. However, it can be adapted for use in a Sunday school setting as well. Here are some suggestions for using this study in a small group and in a Sunday school class:

In a small group

To create a friendly and comfortable atmosphere, it is recommended that you do this study in a home setting. In many cases, the couple that leads the study also serves as host to the group. Sometimes involving another couple as host is a good idea. Choose the option you believe will work best for your group, taking into account factors such as the number of couples participating and the location.

Each session is designed as a ninety-minute study, but we recommend a two-hour block of time. This will allow you to move through each part of the study at a more relaxed pace. However, be sure to keep in mind one of the cardinal rules of a small group: Good groups start *and* end on time. People's time is valuable, and your group will appreciate your being respectful of this.

In a Sunday school class

There are two important adaptations you need to make if you want to use this study in a class setting: (1) The material you cover should focus on the content from the Blueprints section of each session. Blueprints is the heart of each session and is designed to last sixty minutes. (2) Most Sunday school classes are taught in a teacher format instead of a small-group format. If this study will be used in a class setting, the class should adapt to a small-group dynamic. This will involve an interactive, discussion-based format and may also require a class to break into multiple smaller groups (we recommend groups of six to eight people).

What is the best size group?

We recommend from four to eight couples (including you and your spouse). If you have more people interested than you think you can accommodate, consider asking someone else to lead a second group. If you have a large group, you are encouraged at various times in the study to break into smaller subgroups. This helps you cover the material in a timely fashion and allows for optimum interaction and participation within the group.

What about refreshments?

Many groups choose to serve refreshments, which help create an environment of fellowship. If you plan on including refreshments in your study, here are a couple of suggestions: (1) For the first session (or two) you should provide the refreshments and then allow the group to be involved by having people sign up to bring them on later dates. (2) Consider starting your group with a short time of informal fellowship and refreshments (fifteen minutes), then move into the study. If couples are late, they miss only the food and don't disrupt the study. You may also want to have refreshments available at the end of your meeting to encourage fellowship, but remember, respect the group members' time by ending the study on schedule and allowing anyone who needs to leave right away the opportunity to do so gracefully.

What about child care?

Groups handle this differently depending on their needs. Here are a couple of options you may want to consider:

- Have group members be responsible for making their own arrangements.

- As a group, hire child care, and have all the kids watched in one location.

What about prayer?

An important part of a small group is prayer. However, as the leader, you need to be sensitive to the level of comfort the people in your group have toward praying in front of others. Never call on people to pray aloud if you don't know if they are comfortable doing this. There are a number of creative approaches you can take, such as modeling prayer, calling for volunteers, and letting people state their prayers in the form of finishing a sentence. A tool that is helpful in a group is a prayer list. You are encouraged to utilize a prayer list, but let it be someone else's ministry to the group. You should lead the prayer time, but allow another couple in the group the opportunity to create, update, and distribute prayer lists.

In closing

An excellent resource that covers leading a HomeBuilders group in greater detail is the *HomeBuilders Leader Guide* by Drew and Kit Coons. This book may be obtained at your local Christian bookstore or by contacting Group Publishing or FamilyLife.

About the Leader's Notes

The sessions in this study can be easily led without a lot of preparation time. However, accompanying Leader's Notes have been provided to assist you in preparation. The categories within the Leader's Notes are as follows:

Objectives

The purpose of the Objectives is to help focus on the issues that will be presented in each session.

Notes and Tips

This section will relate any general comments about the session. This information should be viewed as ideas, helps, and suggestions. You may want to create a checklist of things you want to be sure to do in each session.

Commentary

Included in this section are notes that relate specifically to Blueprints questions. Not all Blueprints questions in each session will have accompanying commentary notes. Questions with related commentaries are designated by numbers (for example, Blueprints question 8 in Session One would correspond to number 8 in the Commentary section of Session One Leader's Notes).

Session One:

The Basis of Teamwork

Objectives

God's Word provides the foundation upon which teamwork in marriage is built.

In this session, couples will...

• enjoy getting to know other couples.

• consider various elements that make for a good team.

• discuss goals for their marriage.

• identify love as the basis of teamwork in marriage.

Notes and Tips

1. If you have not already done so, you will want to read the information on pages 4 and 5 as well as "About Leading a HomeBuilders Group" and "About the Leader's Notes" starting on page 102.

2. To further equip yourself for leading this course, you may want to get the book *Rocking the Roles: Building a Win-Win Marriage* by Robert Lewis and William Hendricks (NavPress, 1991). This book provides additional information on the topics discussed in this study.

3. As part of the first session, you should review with the group some Ground Rules (see page 9 in the Introduction).

4. Be sure you have a study guide for each person. You will also want to have extra Bibles, and pens or pencils.

5. If this group has not been together before, a fun way to have couples introduce themselves is to have them briefly share how and when they met. Depending on the size of your group, you may end up spending longer than 15 minutes for Warm-Up. If this happens, try to finish Blueprints in 45 to 60 minutes. It is a good idea to mark the questions in Blueprints that you want to be sure to cover. For any questions you don't cover during the session, encourage couples to look at them when they complete the HomeBuilders Project for this session.

6. You will notice a note in the margin at the start of Blueprints that recommends breaking into smaller groups. The reason for this is twofold: (1) to help facilitate discussion and participation by everyone, and (2) to help you cover the material in the allotted time.

7. Question 5 in Blueprints calls for couples to look up different Scripture passages. This procedure lets the group examine multiple passages simultaneously. This saves time and gives group members the opportunity to learn from one another.

Depending on how many couples you have in your group, it's OK for a couple to choose more than one passage or for more than one couple to choose the same passage.

8. Because this is the first session, you may want to offer a closing prayer instead of asking others to pray aloud. Many people are uncomfortable praying in front of others, and unless you already know your group well, it may be wise to slowly venture into various methods of prayer. Regardless of how you decide to close, you should serve as a model. (Note: pages 131 and 132 can be used for the group to record prayer requests.)

9. Because this is the first session, make a special point to tell the group about the importance of the HomeBuilders Project. Encourage each couple to "Make a Date" to complete the project before the next meeting. Mention that during the Warm-Up of the next session, you will ask about the previous week's HomeBuilders Project.

10. This group is just getting under way, so it's not too late to invite another couple to join. Challenge everyone to think about a couple they could invite to the next session.

Commentary

Here is some additional information about various Blueprints questions. The numbers that follow correspond to the Blueprints questions of the same numbers in the session. If you share any of these points, be sure to do so in a manner that does not stifle discussion by making you the authority with *the real answers*. Begin your comments by saying things like, "One thing I notice in this passage is..." or "I think another reason for this is..."

Notes are not included for every question. Many of the questions in this study are designed for group members to draw from their own opinions and experiences.

1. Suggest these responses if the group doesn't come up with something similar: good coaching, knowledge of the sport, and a proper understanding of what is required of each player.

2. Teams with less-gifted players can work effectively as a team to beat a team that has better athletes. Sometimes a team with gifted individuals never finds a way for those players to work well together.

In other words, you don't necessarily need to be the most gifted athlete to win! To illustrate this point, you may want to recall the fable of the tortoise and the hare. Ecclesiastes 9:11 makes a similar point.

3. One of the biggest factors that cause a husband and wife not to work together as a team is our natural selfishness—our desire to go our own way and to be concerned primarily with meeting our own needs.

4. In responding to this question, challenge couples to think about the issues they have faced in their marriage that have required teamwork.

If helpful to the discussion, you may want to mention that typical challenges can include deciding how to divide household tasks, such as cooking, cleaning, and managing finances; figuring how to work well together as parents; and caring for each other in times of sickness and tragedy.

8. If the only goal is to have fun, you may not accomplish much. The players may not learn very much about how to play the game, they may not learn much about teamwork, and you may have a difficult time enforcing discipline.

To win the championship is a challenging goal, but you may be setting up your players for disappointment if this is the only goal—especially with this set of players. Too many factors must fall into place for a team to win a league championship, and many of those factors are out of your control. This may lead to frustration if things don't go well. You may be tempted to be overly harsh with your players. They may feel too much pressure and might not enjoy the season at all.

Some examples of wise and realistic goals could be to teach your team the basic skills of the game, to teach them to play as a team, to make sure every player has a chance to contribute, to strive to play your best in each game, and to have fun while doing so.

11. These passages tell us that the goal of any Christian is to serve and glorify our Father in heaven. We should live our lives in a way that allows God's light to show through us, and we should trust God to provide for our needs.

12. You may want to make the point that if a couple were to adopt these goals, they would have a common purpose in their marriage—working together to glorify God—and their whole perspective on life and marriage would change.

Attention HomeBuilders Leaders

Session Two:
Equal, Yet Different

Objectives

While God has created men and women with unique differences, both have equal worth in Christ.

In this session, couples will...

- identify and discuss basic differences between men and women.

- examine their value and standing before God.

- work to better understand, appreciate, and honor each other's differences.

Notes and Tips

1. One of the subjects this session covers is the difference between men and women. This topic will come up in some of the Warm-Up answers and more directly in question 1 of Blueprints. This topic can be controversial because during the past few decades we've seen an ongoing debate about why men and women are different. Some have maintained that all differences other than obviously physical differences can be explained by how we are raised in our culture. However, mainstream scientific research now seems to agree that, while some differences between men and women are shaped by environment, other differences are part of our very nature.

Encourage a lively discussion on this topic, but keep comments focused on the fact that there are differences, rather than on the source of those differences. In a marriage, it's important to acknowledge, understand, and appreciate differences between a husband and wife, whether those differences are the result of gender or of interests and skills.

2. Because this is the second session, your group members have probably warmed up to each other but may not yet feel free to be open about their relationship. Don't force the issue. Continue to encourage couples to attend the sessions and complete the projects.

3. If a couple joins the group for the first time this session, you will want to introduce them to the other couples. Also, during Warm-Up let them introduce themselves to the group by briefly sharing how and when they met. You should also recap the main points from Session One and have couples record contact information in their books (p. 14).

4. If you told the group during the first session that you would ask them to share something they learned from the first HomeBuilders Project, be sure to ask them. This is an opportunity to establish an environment of accountability.

5. Make sure the arrangements for refreshments (if you're planning to have them) are covered.

6. If your group has decided to use a prayer list, make sure this item is covered.

7. For the closing prayer in this session, you may want to ask for a volunteer or two to close the group in prayer. Check ahead of time with a couple of people you think might be comfortable praying aloud.

Commentary

Note: The numbers that follow correspond to the Blueprints questions of the same numbers in the session.

1. For this question, see point number 1 of the preceding "Notes and Tips."

2. While husbands and wives have historically failed to understand and appreciate their differences, a case could be argued that husbands generally need to be exhorted more strongly in this area.

3. Understanding can come through honest study and discussion. Spouses should talk about their different needs, ways of relating to others, interests, and priorities.

4. Understanding differences helps a husband and wife live and work together. Such understanding can also help a couple recognize and balance each other's strengths and weaknesses. If you don't understand the differences between you and your spouse, you will tend to assume that your spouse thinks, feels, and has the same needs that you do.

6. First Peter 3:7 both recognizes differences (referring to wives as the "weaker partner"), as well as equality (recognizing husbands and wives as partners and co-heirs of the "the gracious gift of life"). As fellow heirs of all that is good in life, a husband and wife should have an equal share of all they experience in marriage.

The phrase "weaker partner" most likely refers to a woman's physical strength as compared to that of a man.

7. Our faith gives us equal standing and equal worth before God. We are heirs of the same promises. If a husband and wife have received Christ as Savior, they have received the same salvation, the same blessings, and can enjoy the same type of relationship with God.

Some people believe that Galatians 3:28 eliminates gender-role distinctions in marriage. However, it seems more likely that Paul is talking here about our salvation in Christ.

8. We all have equal standing before God—in Christ he offers the same forgiveness, the same cleansing of sin to all.

9. If this issue isn't raised in the discussion, mention that this view will affect how one spouse treats the other. Such a view also reflects how a spouse regards the responsibilities that each partner has to create a working team in the marriage.

10. While the most immediate application of 1 Corinthians 12:12-26 is to the church, it is also very easy in marriage to believe that some functions and gifts are superior to others. Yet this passage presents the crucial principle that, even though each of us has a different gift or function, all of us are equally important in the kingdom of God. No matter what function we have in marriage, we have equal worth before God.

Session Three:
Following Christ's Example

Objectives

To rightly relate to one another as husband and wife, we need to follow Christ's example of serving others.

In this session, couples will...

- study the example Christ set for serving others.

- learn more about each others needs.

- commit to a specific way to serve each other.

Notes and Tips

1. Congratulations! With the completion of this session, you will be halfway through this study. It's time for a checkup: How are you feeling? How is the group going? What has worked well so far? What things might you consider changing as you approach the remaining sessions?

2. Greet people as they arrive for the session. Share personal expressions of appreciation for people's participation and support in earlier sessions. Tell people of your appreciation for the opportunity to get to know them better.

3. Remember the importance of starting and ending the session on time.

4. As an example to the group, it is important that you and your spouse complete the HomeBuilders Project each session.

5. *For Extra Impact:* Before starting the Blueprints questions for this session, demonstrate Christ-like servanthood by washing the feet of the people in your group. If you have a particularly large group, you may want to wash only one person's feet. (Your spouse would be a good candidate; however, for maximum effect, this act of service should be a surprise.) Do this quietly without an announcement. Expect resistance; resistance is part of the experience.

After the foot-washing experience, read John 13:1-17. Debrief the experience as a group by discussing the following questions:

• What emotions did you experience during this act?

• How was your reaction like or unlike Peter's? (Or, if you washed only one person's feet for this activity, ask the group: How do you think your reaction might have been like or unlike that of the person whose feet were washed?)

• What was Jesus trying to teach the disciples by washing their feet?

6. If you do the recommended "For Extra Impact" activity, by-pass questions 1-3 in Blueprints. You may also want to go through the remaining Blueprints questions and mark questions that you want to cover. If you don't finish all of the questions during the session, suggest that group members answer the remaining questions when they complete this session's HomeBuilders Project.

Commentary

Note: The numbers that follow correspond to the Blueprints questions of the same numbers in the session.

1. Jesus is teaching about the importance of being a servant. Washing feet was a task relegated to servants.

2. Peter regarded Jesus as his master, so he was shocked that Jesus actually wanted to wash his feet. In Peter's mind, being a leader meant that others washed your feet, not vice versa.

3. Throughout his ministry, Jesus served those who followed him and sought to meet their needs. He continually pointed them toward God and trained them in how to minister to others to glorify the Father.

5. Christ's idea of leadership is a radically different concept of leadership. The world bestows power, privilege, praise, wealth, and status to its leaders. And those leaders often take advantage of others to bolster their standing. However, Jesus says leaders should be servants.

Some people might have difficulty reconciling serving with leading. You may need to state several times that almost everything in our society conditions us to view these terms as opposites. Jesus was truly revolutionary when he linked them together.

8. When you look only to your own interests in your relationship, you will grow isolated from each other.

Session Four:
Biblical Responsibilities

Objectives

The Bible sets forth key responsibilities for husbands and wives.

In this session, couples will...

- recognize that God has given certain unique responsibilities to husbands and wives.

- examine scriptural instructions about the key responsibilities of husbands and wives.

- define what they see as their key biblical responsibilities.

Notes and Tips

1. This session tackles an issue that can be controversial—responsibilities of husbands and wives. Couples may not have a clear understanding of what the Bible says on this subject and may have preconceived ideas. Over the past few decades in our culture, the biblical models of responsibilities in marriage have been attacked, stereotyped, and ridiculed.

Some people will have no problem accepting what the Bible says about the subject of biblical responsibilities, but others may. Your goal is to encourage the group members to set aside preconceived notions and take an honest look at what these Scriptures mean and how to apply them in marriage.

While this session examines passages related to biblical responsibilities of husbands and wives, it does not attempt to deal with every responsibility in marriage addressed in the Bible. Rather, this session provides a general overview of what the Bible says and avoids specific issues such as child-rearing and physical intimacy. The goal is to lay a foundation of understanding, challenging husbands and wives to consider their overall responsibilities in marriage.

It's important to remember that to fully comprehend what the Bible says about responsibilities in marriage, you must first understand the biblical foundations discussed in the first three sessions. For example, the discussion in the last session about true biblical leadership sets the stage for a discussion in this session about leadership in marriage.

2. Be prepared for the discussion in this session to go long. Here are a couple of options: Look through all the questions beforehand and mark the ones you want to be sure to discuss, or suggest to the group the option of finishing the discussion during your next meeting.

3. During Warm-Up, you may want to ask who followed through with the Wrap-Up activity from Session 3 and how spouses responded to the act of service from their spouse.

4. Because of the subject being discussed, it is quite possible for a group to spend a lot of time discussing one question. Be wary of stifling good dialog; however, it is important for you to politely keep things moving forward. In particular, be sure to allow time for the last Blueprints question. This is a key point of application for husbands and wives.

5. You and your spouse may want to write notes of thanks and encouragement to the couples in your group this week. Thank them for their commitment and contribution to the group, and let them know that you are praying for them. Make a point to pray for them as you write their note.

Commentary

1. For the subgroups used with this question, consider breaking into groups of husbands and wives.

Note: The numbers that follow correspond to the Blueprints questions of the same numbers in the session.

2. The exact definition of "head" in relation to its use in Ephesians 5:23 is in debate among scholars. "Whether Paul intends the term to mean an authoritative ruler, or the first in a series, leader, servant-leader, or some other sense of 'head' is left open to debate. Of course, one important way of determining a metaphor's meaning is to check the surrounding context. Context along with other biblical references strongly suggest the servant-leader interpretation, in the authors' opinion." (*Rocking the Roles: Building a Win-Win Marriage*, Robert Lewis and William Hendricks, NavPress, 1991)

Historically, it should be noted that Paul's statement in Ephesians 5:23 is not drawn from a culture where men reigned unchallenged as heads of their women. In fact, a serious breakdown of marriage and family was occurring throughout the Roman Empire at this time.

3. Throughout history, many husbands have misunderstood the concept of headship and have used it for selfish means. They have used it as an instrument of power and control and have subjugated their wives to various degrees. They have used the concept as the foundation for believing that men are superior to women. At the extreme, some have abused their wives emotionally and physically. This is not what the Bible teaches.

Some people cite the failure of husbands in properly exercising biblical headship as a reason to reject the entire idea of unique responsibilities in marriage. But the tendency for people to disobey, misunderstand, and distort the Scriptures does not mean that those Scriptures are not God's truth.

4. Christ's example of servanthood should serve to cast leadership in marriage in a fresh perspective.

5. You may want to challenge people to think about their experiences with various authority figures and what styles of leadership they have reacted against.

6. This kind of love reflects an attitude of profound selflessness and humility; a willingness to sacrifice yourself for another.

8. It is interesting to note that "helper" is a title that God applies to himself. The use of the term "helper" is a more lofty title in Scripture than what is typically assigned to it in the context of our society.

10. If the group's discussion does not bring up this interpretation, you may want to share the interpretation that this phrase speaks of the need for a wife to make her home a priority.

11. These verses should not be read as contradicting each other; rather, they reveal great flexibility in how a woman

fulfills her responsibilities as a wife and mother. The
Proverbs 31 woman focuses on honoring her husband and
caring for her family, yet she also buys a field, plants a vine-
yard, trades goods, and helps the poor.

12. The biblical responsibilities of a husband include sacrifi-
cial servant-leadership. The biblical responsibilities of a
wife include supporting her husband and making the home a
priority.

Session Five:
Biblical Responses

Objectives

A husband and wife can help each other fulfill their biblical responsibilities by how they respond to one another.

In this session, couples will...

- recognize the importance of how they respond to their spouse.

- examine what the Bible says their response should be.

- define what they see as their biblical response.

- discuss how they can support and encourage one another.

Notes and Tips

1. This session raises a topic that can be controversial—the issue of a wife's "submission" in marriage. It's difficult for many people to set aside preconceived ideas on this subject, and you probably will have a spirited discussion. It's important to keep the topic centered on the Scriptures. As with other difficult subjects in the Bible, we need to look at how to understand and apply what the Scripture says, even when we may not like it. And remember that this concept cannot be understood apart from the context of the subjects we studied in the first three sessions.

2. Be prepared for the discussion to go long on some questions. Look through all the questions beforehand and mark the ones you want to be sure to discuss.

3. As the leader of a small group, one of the best things you can do for your group is to pray specifically for each group member. Take some time to pray as you prepare for this session.

4. *Looking ahead:* For the next session—the last session of this study—you may want to ask someone, or a couple, to share what this study or group has meant to them. If you would like to do this, be thinking about who you will ask to share.

5. You may find it helpful to make some notes right after the meeting to help you evaluate how this session went. Ask yourself questions such as: Did everyone participate? Do I need to make a special effort to follow up with anyone before the next session? Asking yourself such questions will help you stay focused.

Commentary

1. The word "submission" comes from Greek words that mean "under" and "arrange." The sense of the term is to voluntarily organize or fit under.

Note: The numbers that follow correspond to the Blueprints questions of the same numbers in the session.

3. Submission should be voluntary. A husband who criticizes his wife for not being submissive may not be fulfilling his own responsibilities as a servant-leader in the marriage.

4. Following are some common questions that are often raised about submission, along with some Scriptures:

- What if a Christian wife is married to a nonChristian husband? See 1 Peter 3:1-2.

- How should a wife respond to a husband's inconsistencies and failures? See Colossians 3:12-13 and Galatians 6:1.

- What if a husband wants me to do something wrong or illegal? See Acts 5:29.

The Bible does not ask wives to submit to sinful or damaging demands. A husband who is fulfilling his biblical responsibilities will not ask or pressure his wife to violate scriptural commands. A husband's leadership is meant to fulfill Scripture, not violate it.

In the case of mistreatment or abuse, professional help should be sought immediately.

Here's another question that may be raised in the discussion on submission: What if a wife is at times mistreated? In the case of mistreatment or abuse, professional help should be sought immediately. There is nothing in Scripture to support the idea that "submission" requires women to allow their husbands to abuse them or to abuse their children.

7. To add to the impact of this question, you may want to look at these verses from multiple Bible translations.

9. Because we live in a world that equates "submission" with inferiority, a wife needs praise and honor to help build her up and encourage her. Note: This principle may provide a revolutionary insight for some men and women in your group. While we often hear exhortations for wives to submit, we rarely hear about the masculine counterpart of honor and praise.

10. Beyond the obvious negative effects to the wife, such as low self-esteem, the marriage will not be healthy and could be in danger. Also, the husband hurts himself by missing out on the blessings that come from being a God-honoring husband.

12. Praise and honor is a husband's biblical response to his wife. Submission is a wife's spiritual response to her husband.

Session Six:
Making Teamwork Work

Objectives

Through the power of the Holy Spirit, you can apply the principles of teamwork in your marriage.

In this session, couples will...

- apply biblical responsibilities and responses to real-life scenarios.

- recognize their need for God's help in building teamwork in marriage.

- reflect on and evaluate their experience with this course.

Notes and Tips

1. Some of the Blueprints questions in this session revolve around the Holy Spirit. If you sense that this is an unfamiliar subject for anyone in your group, you may want to spend some time explaining who the Holy Spirit is and how the Spirit works in a Christian's life. A good way of explaining the Holy Spirit is to share experiences from your own life.

On a related note, if you believe someone in your group has questions about what a Christian is, this might be a good time to take a few minutes to explain how you became a Christian and the difference that Christ has made in your life.

You can also refer group members to the article "Our

Problems, God's Answers" (p. 91) for more information about these subjects.

2. While this HomeBuilders Couples Series has great value, people are likely to return to previous patterns of living unless they commit to a plan for carrying on the progress made through the study. During this final session of the course, encourage couples to take specific steps beyond this series to keep their marriages growing. For example, you may want to challenge couples who have developed the habit of a "date night" during the course of this study to continue this practice. Also, you may want the group to consider completing another study from this series.

3. As a part of this final session, you may want to devote some time to plan for one more meeting—a party to celebrate the completion of this study!

Commentary

7. The Holy Spirit is our guide and helps us understand Scripture and discern the will of God. Also, notice the prepositions used in John 14:16 and 17: First, the Holy Spirit will "be *with* you forever," and "will be *in* you." These words indicate our relationship with the Holy Spirit is meant to be a very intimate one.

Note: The numbers that follow correspond to the Blueprints questions of the same numbers in the session.

8. During this course you have studied God's Word and learned how it applies to different areas of your marriage. In John 14:15-26, Jesus says that the proof of our love for him will

be found in our obedience to his commands. He then promises us the Holy Spirit, who will live within us and act as our Counselor. The Holy Spirit will remind us of everything God teaches us in his Word and will give us the power to obey it as we face different circumstances in our marriage.

You may want to be prepared to share a personal example of how the Holy Spirit has worked in your marriage.

9. Because our sinful nature is hostile to God's law, our sinful nature will influence us to disobey the Bible.

11. Living by the Spirit means a continual dependence on the Holy Spirit for wisdom, guidance, and power. As an act of our will, we need to choose to yield to the influence of God's Spirit.

Prayer Requests

Prayer Requests

FamilyLife has been presenting couples with the wonderful news of God's blueprints for marriage since 1976. Today we are strengthening hundreds of thousands of homes each year in the United States and around the world through:

◆ **Weekend to Remember** conferences

◆ **One-day arena events** for couples

◆ **HomeBuilders Couples Series®** and **HomeBuilders Parenting Series®** small-group Bible studies

◆ **"FamilyLife Today,"** the daily, half-hour radio program, and four other nationally syndicated broadcasts

◆ A comprehensive Web site, **www.familylife.com**, featuring marriage and parenting tips, daily devotions, conference information, and a wide range of resources for strengthening families

◆ Unique marriage and family **connecting resources**

Through these outreaches, FamilyLife is effectively developing godly families who reach the world one home at a time.

FAMILYLIFE™
Bringing Timeless Principles Home

Dennis Rainey, President
1-800-FL-TODAY (358-6329)
www.familylife.com
A division of Campus Crusade for Christ

Does Your Church Offer Marriage Insurance?

Great marriages don't just happen—husbands and wives need to nurture them. They need to make their marriage relationship a priority.

That's where the newly revised HomeBuilders Couples Series® can help! The series consists of interactive 6- to 7-week small group studies that make it easy for couples to really open up with each other. The result is fun, non-threatening interactions that build stronger Christ-centered relationships between spouses—and with other couples!

Whether you've been married for years, or are newly married, this series will help you and your spouse discover timeless principles from God's Word that you can apply to your marriage and make it the best it can be!

The HomeBuilders Leader Guide gives you all the information and encouragement you need to start and lead a dynamic HomeBuilders small group.

The HomeBuilders Couples Series includes these life-changing studies:
- Building Teamwork in Your Marriage
- Building Your Marriage *(also available in Spanish!)*
- Building Your Mate's Self-Esteem
- Growing Together in Christ
- Improving Communication in Your Marriage *(also available in Spanish!)*
- Making Your Remarriage Last
- Mastering Money in Your Marriage
- Overcoming Stress in Your Marriage
- Resolving Conflict in Your Marriage

And check out the HomeBuilders Parenting series!
- Building Character in Your Children
- Establishing Effective Discipline for Your Children
- Guiding Your Teenagers
- Helping Your Children Know God
- Improving Your Parenting
- Raising Children of Faith

Look for the **HomeBuilders Couples Series and HomeBuilders Parenting Series** at your favorite Christian supplier or write:

P.O. Box 485, Loveland, CO 80539-0485.
www.grouppublishing.com

FAMILYLIFE™
Bringing Timeless Principles Home

www.familylife.com